THE STORY OF EARTH

By NADIA HIGGINS

Illustrations by JIA LIU

Music by JOSEPH FAISON IV

CANTATA
LEARNING

WWW.CANTATALEARNING.COM

CANTATA LEARNING

Published by Cantata Learning
1710 Roe Crest Drive
North Mankato, MN 56003
www.cantatalearning.com

Library of Congress Cataloging-in-Publication Data
Names: Higgins, Nadia, author. | Liu, Jia (Illustrator), illustrator. |
Faison, Joseph, IV, composer.
Title: The story of Earth / by Nadia Higgins ; illustrated by Jia Liu ; music
by Joseph Faison IV.
Description: North Mankato, MN : Cantata Learning, [2018] | Series: What
shapes our Earth? | Includes lyrics and sheet music. | Audience: Ages 6–9.
| Audience: K to grade 3.
Identifiers: LCCN 2017017524 (print) | LCCN 2017031544 (ebook) | ISBN
9781684101726 (ebook) | ISBN 9781684101290 (hardcover : alk. paper)
Subjects: LCSH: Children's songs, English. | Earth (Planet)--Juvenile
literature.
Classification: LCC QB631.4 (ebook) | LCC QB631.4 .H54 2018 (print) | DDC
525--dc23
LC record available at https://lccn.loc.gov/2017017524

Book design and art direction, Tim Palin Creative
Editorial direction, Kellie M. Hultgren
Music direction, Elizabeth Draper
Music arranged and produced by Joseph Faison IV

Printed in the United States of America in North Mankato, Minnesota.
122017   0378CGS18

ACCESS THE MUSIC!

SCAN CODE WITH MOBILE APP

CANTATALEARNING.COM

TIPS TO SUPPORT LITERACY AT HOME

WHY READING AND SINGING WITH YOUR CHILD IS SO IMPORTANT

Daily reading with your child leads to increased academic achievement. Music and songs, specifically rhyming songs, are a fun and easy way to build early literacy and language development. Music skills correlate significantly with both phonological awareness and reading development. Singing helps build vocabulary and speech development. And reading and appreciating music together is a wonderful way to strengthen your relationship.

READ AND SING EVERY DAY!

TIPS FOR USING CANTATA LEARNING BOOKS AND SONGS DURING YOUR DAILY STORY TIME

1. As you sing and read, point out the different words on the page that rhyme. Suggest other words that rhyme.

2. Memorize simple rhymes such as Itsy Bitsy Spider and sing them together. This encourages comprehension skills and early literacy skills.

3. Use the questions in the back of each book to guide your singing and storytelling.

4. Read the included sheet music with your child while you listen to the song. How do the music notes correlate to the words of the song?

5. Sing along on the go and at home. Access music by scanning the QR code on each Cantata book, or by using the included CD. You can also stream or download the music for free to your computer, smartphone, or mobile device.

Devoting time to daily reading shows that you are available for your child. Together, you are building language, literacy, and listening skills.

Have fun reading and singing!

Earth formed a long, long time ago from a cloud of dust. Early on, our planet was a pretty scary place! Slowly but surely, it got better. After **billions** of years, life took off. Our planet became the home we know and love.

Turn the page. Sing your heart out to the story of Earth!

Eons ago, time before time,
before rocks, wind, and warm sunshine,
a huge cloud of dust spun and swirled.
It slowly formed into our world.

Our planet was not always blue,
with forests green and mountain views.

Through billions of years it came to be
a home just right for you and me.

Early Earth was steaming hot,
a sloshing sea of liquid rock.

No air to breathe, no clouds up high,
and space rocks crashing from the sky!

Our planet was not always blue
with forests green and mountain views.

Through billions of years it came to be
a home just right for you and me.

Eventually, Earth settled down
with mountains, seas, and solid ground.

Tiny life forms **evolved**, and then
they filled the air with **oxygen**.

16

The oceans filled with fish and clams.
Then plants began to grow on land.

Mighty dinosaurs ruled for an age.
Much later, humans took the stage.

Earth is changing. It's still shifting.
Lands are joining, lands are drifting.

Mountains grow and rivers fade.
The story of Earth is still being made.

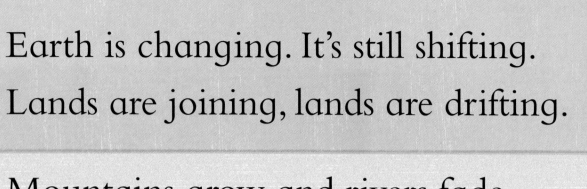

Our planet was not always blue,
with forests green and mountain views.

Through billions of years it came to be
a home just right for you and me.

A home just right for you and me!

21

SONG LYRICS
The Story of Earth

Eons ago, time before time,
before rocks, wind, and warm sunshine,
a huge cloud of dust spun and swirled.
It slowly formed into our world.

Our planet was not always blue,
with forests green and mountain views.
Through billions of years it came to be
a home just right for you and me.

Early Earth was steaming hot,
a sloshing sea of liquid rock.
No air to breathe, no clouds up high,
and space rocks crashing from the sky!

Our planet was not always blue
with forests green and mountain views.
Through billions of years it came to be
a home just right for you and me.

Eventually, Earth settled down
with mountains, seas, and solid ground.
Tiny life forms evolved, and then
they filled the air with oxygen.

The oceans filled with fish and clams.
Then plants began to grow on land.
Mighty dinosaurs ruled for an age.
Much later, humans took the stage.

Earth is changing. It's still shifting.
Lands are joining, lands are drifting.
Mountains grow and rivers fade.
The story of Earth is still being made.

Our planet was not always blue,
with forests green and mountain views.
Through billions of years it came to be
a home just right for you and me.

A home just right for you and me!

The Story of Earth

Americana
Joseph Faison IV

Verse

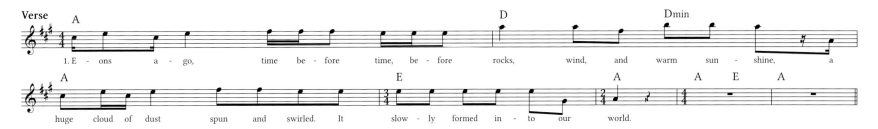

1. E - ons a - go, time be - fore time, be - fore rocks, wind, and warm sun - shine, a

huge cloud of dust spun and swirled. It slow - ly formed in - to our world.

Chorus

Our plan - et was not al - ways blue, with for - ests green and moun - tain views. Through bil - lions of years it came to be a

home just right for you and me. me. a home just right for you and me.

Interlude

Verse 2
Early Earth was steaming hot,
a sloshing sea of liquid rock.
No air to breathe, no clouds up high,
and space rocks crashing from the sky!

Chorus

Interlude

Verse 3
Eventually, Earth settled down
with mountains, seas, and solid ground.
Tiny life forms evolved, and then
they filled the air with oxygen.

Verse 4
The oceans filled with fish and clams.
Then plants began to grow on land.
Mighty dinosaurs ruled for an age.
Much later, humans took the stage.

Bridge

Earth is chang - ing. It's still shift - ing. Lands are join - ing, lands are drift - ing. Moun - tains grow and riv - ers fade. The sto - ry of Earth is still be - ing made.

Chorus

GLOSSARY

billion—a large number that has nine zeroes; a billion equals a thousand millions

eon—a very long period of time

evolved—changed slowly over a very long time

oxygen—a gas in the air that animals and plants need to live

GUIDED READING ACTIVITIES

1. What is your very favorite place on Earth? Draw a picture.

2. Listen to the song again. Every time you hear the word *planet*, make a big circle with your arms. Every time you hear the word *Earth*, give yourself a hug.

3. Draw a line. Use a ruler to make it 8 inches long. Now mark each inch. Imagine this line shows the time since Earth formed. Circle the seventh mark. That's how long it was before animals showed up.

TO LEARN MORE

Aston, Dianna Hutts. *A Rock Is Lively*. Mankato, MN: Amicus, 2014.

Bullard, Lisa. *Earth Day Every Day*. Minneapolis: Millbrook, 2012.

Hunter, Nick. *Earth*. Chicago: Raintree, 2013.

Rake, Matthew. *The Dawn of Planet Earth*. Minneapolis: Hungry Tomato, 2016.